STARRY
NIGHT,
BLURRY
DREAMS

Henn Kim

Andrews McMeel
PUBLISHING®

Waiting for the Night

bad day

7

across the universe

tea time

I'm waiting for the night

no matter how hard
keep thinking sharp

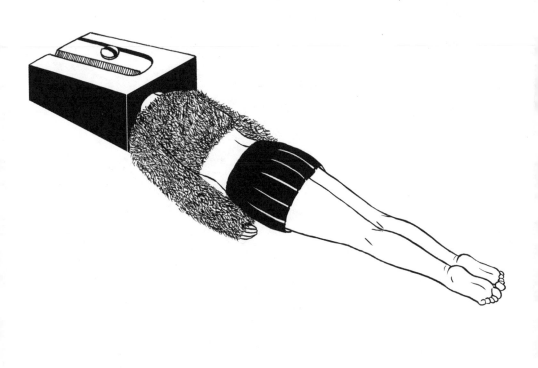

how fragile we are

erase the pain

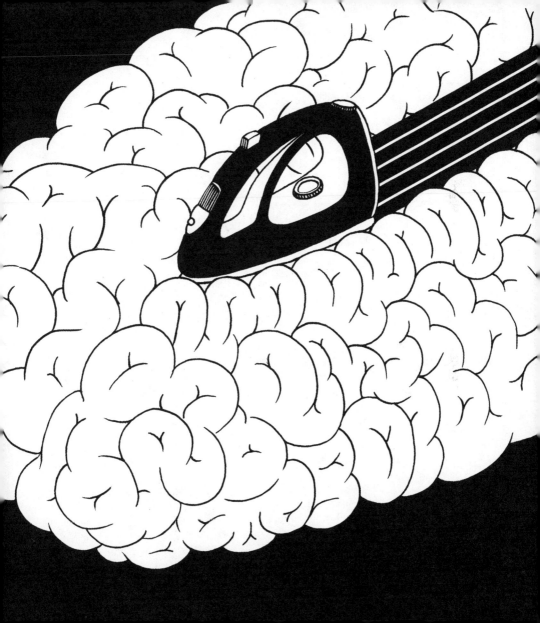

tucked up in tears

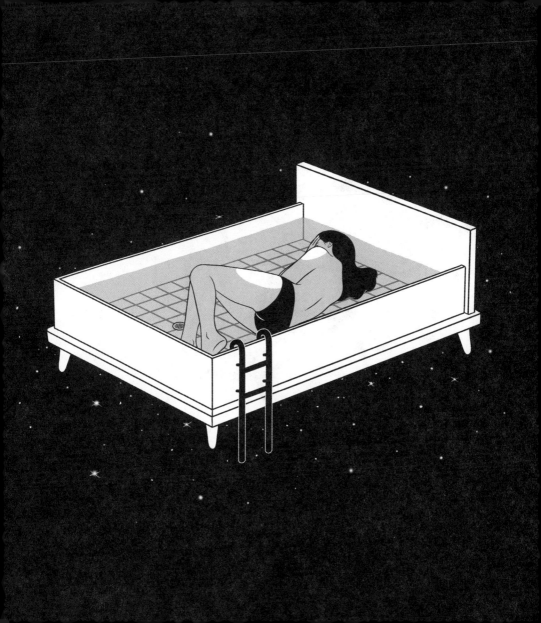

dry your tears

a big hug for you

big girls don't cry

laid-back time

sunday chilling

I need a vacation
from my life

wanderlust

cheers for tears

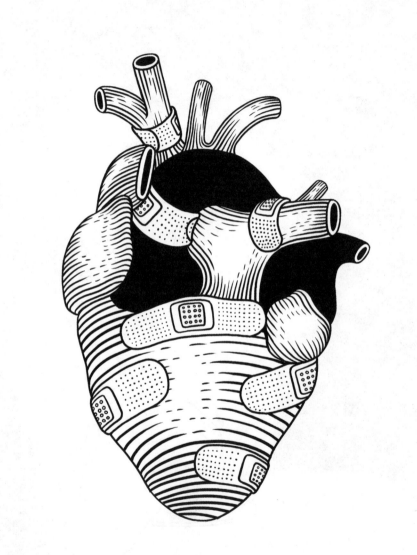

it's hurtful
to be heartful

rebirth

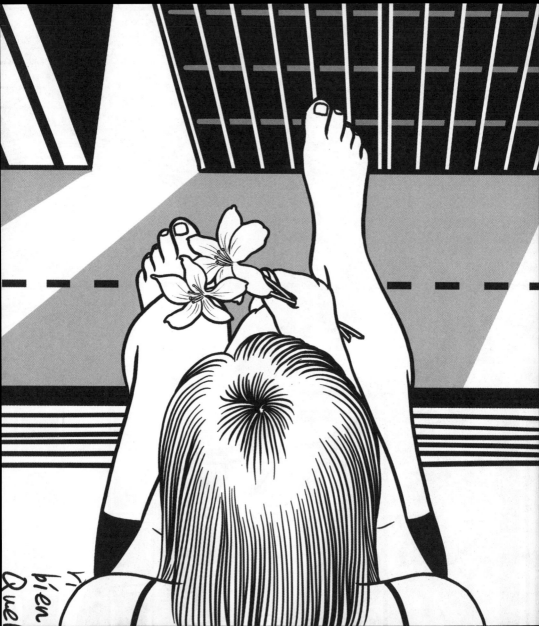

the end of the story

nobody knows the real me

the daily storm
in my unquiet heart

morning, please don't come

hard to move on,
easily swinging

let me bloom

washing away the bad memories

a heavy heart is hard to carry
hold on

hangover

hang in there

girls just wanna have fun

I'm nobody

Henn Kim

sometimes I feel like
everyone hates me

everybody hurts

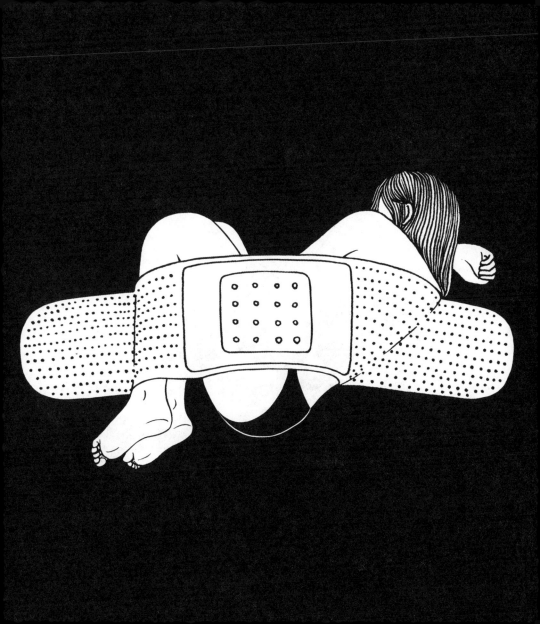

drowning in my own shadow

drenched through my mind

charge me up

say goodbye to the old me
bye

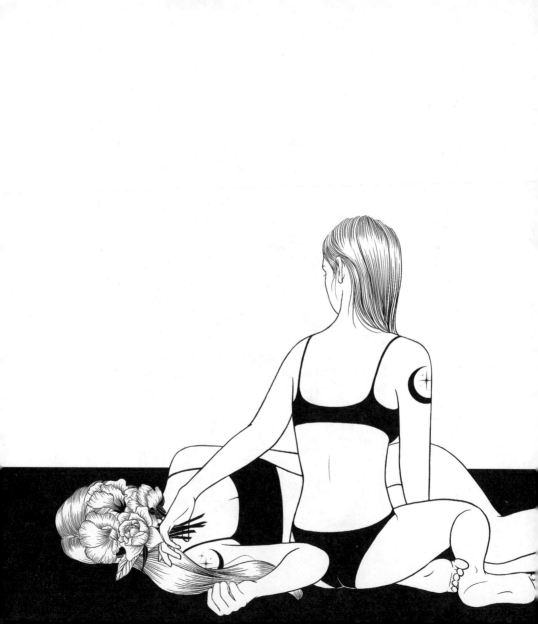

wish I could be part of your world

there are so many things
I want to say

don't think too much

don't stop the lullaby

who are you
when you're alone

to calm my mind
books are my cup of tea

light my fire

cappuccino bath

I'm not crazy, I'm hurt

don't kill my vibe

caution: out of order

to read is to dream

too young to die

we all have our own
beautiful universe

fall in love with myself first

watering the ego

love myself too

You and Me

love song

my little sweetheart

we'll let it burn

rest inside you

time with you runs out
too soon

love you so much

want to be locked with you

I want to know you

fall in love

come into my world

wake up call

a man in love

vision of you

exploring you

do you know
when I'm thinking about you?

rowing to you

we're dreamers

time stands still
when I'm with you

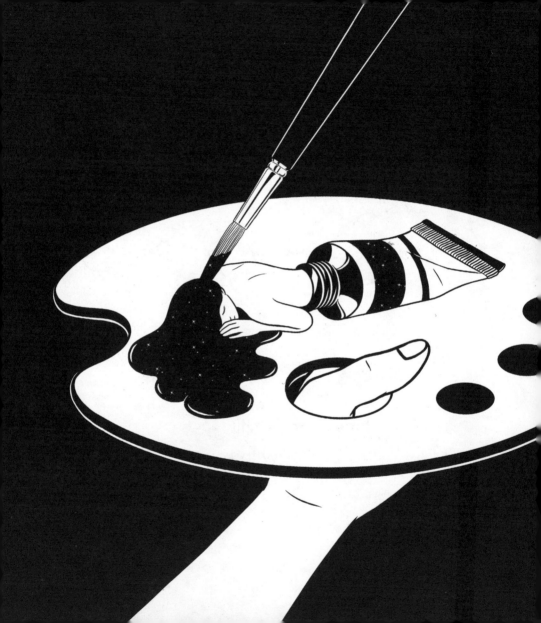

you're my favorite color

ring my bell

sense and sensibility

read all about you

knives to meet you

waiting for your call

never let me go

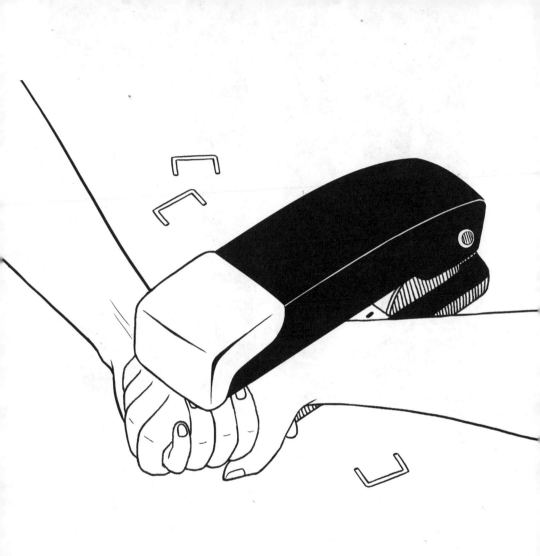

love triangle

finding our way

do I love you or
do I just love me in love

the more I love,
the more I suffer

I hate you
please don't leave me

we light up the dark

energy saving mode
until you charge me again

the closer I get, the harder it is

I'm not ready for the final cut

instant love

breakfast included

summer love
always hurts

dream a little dream of me

how sweet it is

till the love runs out

long-term relationship

Good Night

good night

I don't want to be here
take me with you

escape from reality

take me to wonderland

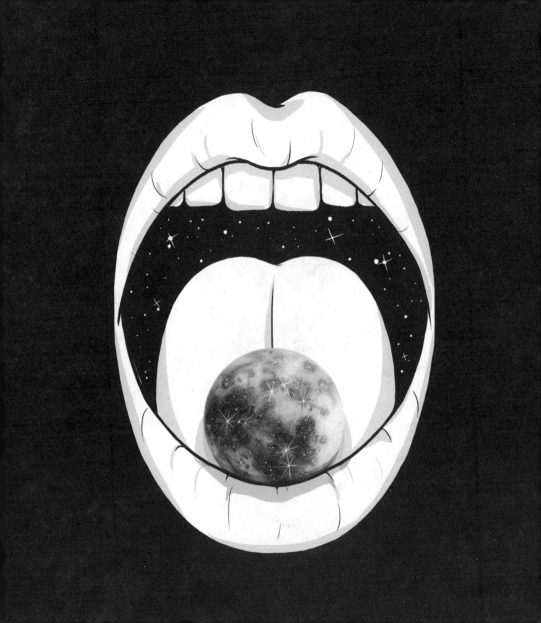

sleeping pill

night flight

flying in the ocean,
swimming in the sky

moon lover

I just got hooked

fly me to the moon

contact

three-minute galaxy

moon river

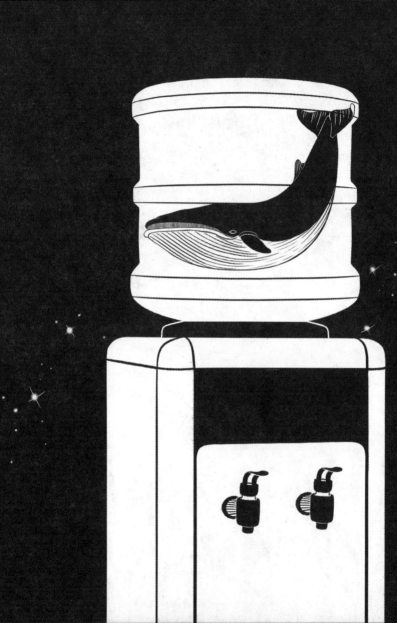

thirst for freedom

dying to live

my little sweet summer

dancing in the rain

take me to the ocean

wild and free

a midsummer night's dream

Sunday Mood

sunday mood

reborn every morning

a natural woman

wake up

good morning!

first, coffee

morning pour over

morning swim

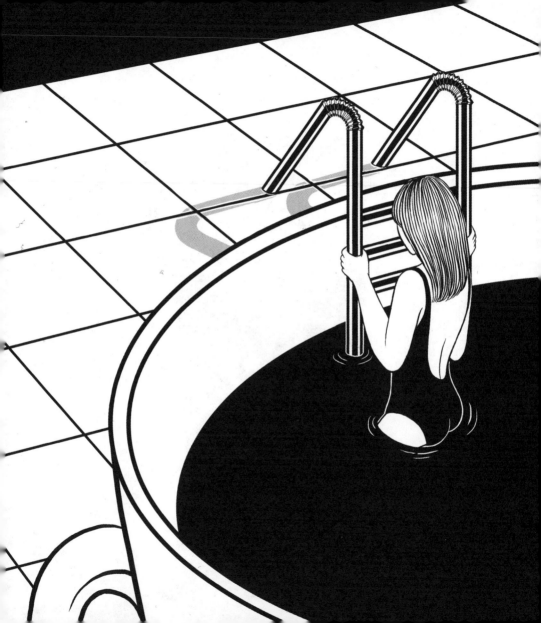

i'm livin' it

every day I'm livin' it

big breakfast

cinema paradiso

selfie

I'm melting

summer and friends

sunny-side up

radio head

soul food

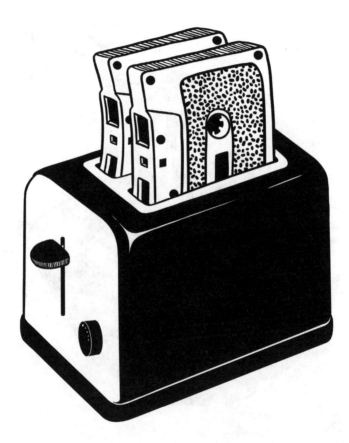

hot music

don't just listen,
feel it

one-minute tan

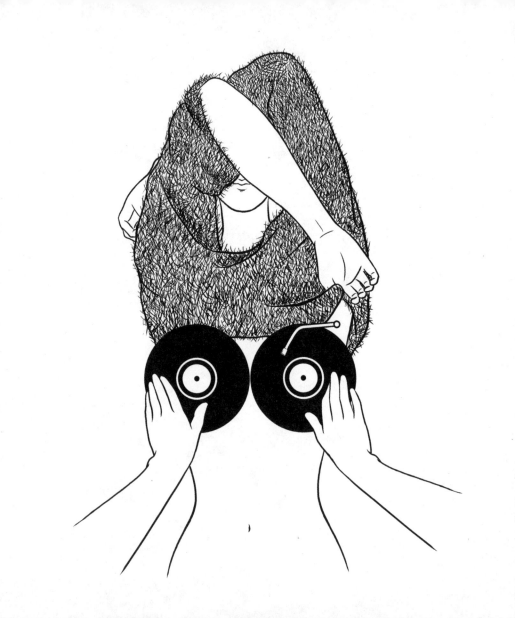

spinning

fresh air

octopus salon

sweet pair

lady grey tea

Van Gogh

art almighty

art addiction

what a wonderful world

my story

Andrews McMeel Publishing
a division of Andrews McMeel Universal
1130 Walnut Street, Kansas City, Missouri 64106

www.andrewsmcmeel.com

Starry Night, Blurry Dreams was originally published
in the UK in 2021 by Bloomsbury Publishing.

22 23 24 25 26 VEP 10 9 8 7 6 5 4 3 2 1

ISBN: 978-1-5248-7133-8

Library of Congress Control Number: 2021949167

ATTENTION: SCHOOLS AND BUSINESSES
Andrews McMeel books are available at quantity discounts
with bulk purchase for educational, business, or sales
promotional use. For information, please e-mail the
Andrews McMeel Publishing Special Sales Department:
specialsales@amuniversal.com.